Look to This Day!

Look to this day!
For it is life, the very life of life.
In its brief course lie all the verities
and realities of your existence:
The bliss of growth;
The glory of action;
The splendor of beauty;
For yesterday is already a dream,
and tomorrow is only a vision;
But today, well lived, makes every yesterday
A dream of happiness, and every tomorrow
a vision of hope.
Look well, therefore, to this day!

from the Sanskrit

An *ideals* Publication

ACKNOWLEDGMENTS

THE FRUIT OF THE SPIRIT IS . . . by Herbert B. Barks. From WORDS ARE NO GOOD AT THE GAME OF SOLITAIRE by Herbert B. Barks. Copyright 1971 by Word, Inc. Used by permission. I WILL NOT HURRY by Ralph S. Cushman. From I HAVE A STEWARDSHIP by Ralph S. Cushman. Copyright renewal 1967 by Maud E. Cushman. Used by permission of Abingdon Press. MOON COMPASSES by Robert Frost. From THE POETRY OF ROBERT FROST edited by Edward Connery Lathem. Copyright 1936 by Robert Frost. Copyright © 1964 by Lesley Frost Ballantine. Copyright © 1969 by Holt, Rinehart and Winston. Reprinted by permission of Holt, Rinehart and Winston, Publishers. THE ROAD NOT TAKEN by Robert Frost. From THE POETRY OF ROBERT FROST edited by Edward Connery Lathem. Copyright 1916, © 1969 by Holt, Rinehart and Winston. Copyright 1944 by Robert Frost. Reprinted by permission of Holt, Rinehart and Winston, Publishers. PIED BEAUTY by Gerard Manley Hopkins. From MODERN VERSE IN ENGLISH 1900-1950 published by Oxford University Press, Inc. POSSESSION by Jane Merchant. From HALFWAY UP THE SKY by Jane Merchant. Published by Abingdon Press. Used through courtesy of Elizabeth Merchant. Excerpt from "Prayer for Peace" from A THOMAS MERTON READER, edited by Thomas P. McDonnell. (Harcourt, Brace Jovanovich, N.Y.) Copyright © 1962 by The Abbey of Gethsemani, Inc. Reprinted by permission of New Directions Publishing Corporation for The Merton Legacy Trust. FOR GREAT MOMENTS by Thomas Merton. From A THOMAS MERTON READER, edited by Thomas P. McDonnell. Copyright © 1962 by The Abbey of Gethsemani, Inc. Reprinted by permission of New Directions Publishing Corporation for the Trustees of the Merton Legacy Trust. "To Build Up Faith" from I'VE GOT TO TALK TO SOMEONE, GOD, Copyright © 1968, 1969 by Marjorie Holmes Mighell. Reprinted by permission of Doubleday & Company, Inc. MIRACLE OF LOVE by Rainer Maria Rilke. Selection is reprinted from LETTERS OF RAINER MARIA RILKE, 1892-1910, Translated by Jane Bannard Greene and M. D. Herter Norton, with the permission of W. W. Norton & Company, Inc. Copyright 1945 by W. W. Norton & Company, Inc. Copyright renewed 1972 by M. D. Herter Norton. "The Waking," copyright 1953 by Theodore Roethke from THE COLLECTED POEMS OF THEODORE ROETHKE. Reprinted by permission of Doubleday & Company, Inc. AFTERNOON ON A HILL and GOD'S WORLD by Edna St. Vincent Millay. From COLLECTED POEMS, Harper & Row. Copyright, 1917, 1945, by Edna St. Vincent Millay and Norma Millay Ellis. "O World" is reprinted by permission of Charles Scribner's Sons from POEMS by George Santayana, copyright 1933 Charles Scribner's Sons. THIS MORNING by Anne Springsteen. From IT'S ME, O LORD, by Anne Springsteen, copyright 1970 by Concordia Publishing House. Used by permission. EVENSONG by Robert Louis Stevenson. From SONGS OF TRAVEL by Robert Louis Stevenson. (Charles Scribner's Sons). BARTER by Sara Teasdale. Reprinted with permission of Macmillan Publishing Co., Inc. from COLLECTED POEMS by Sara Teasdale. Copyright 1917 by Macmillan Publishing Co., Inc., renewed 1945 by Mamie T. Wheless. "A Mile With Me" is reprinted by permission of Charles Scribner's Sons from THE POEMS OF HENRY VAN DYKE. Copyright 1911 Charles Scribner's Sons; renewal copyright 1939 Tertius van Dyke. FOR WISDOM by Viney Wilder. Copyrighted. Used through courtesy of Warp Publishing Co. Our sincere thanks to the following authors whose addresses we were unable to locate: Louise Driscoll for HOLD FAST YOUR DREAMS; Lura Bailey Jones for SUPPLICATION; A. W. Spalding for HIGH ADVENTURE.

ISBN 0-89542-052-X 395

Published by Ideals Publishing Corporation
11315 Watertown Plank Road
Milwaukee, Wis. 53226

Editorial Director, James Kuse
Managing Editor, Ralph Luedtke
Production Manager/Editor, Richard Lawson
Photographic Editor, Gerald Koser

Designed by Patricia Pingry

Look to This Day!

Look to This Day!

—in prayer

This Morning

Life has begun again, Father.

You have given me another day of grace,
another day to live;
   to speak to someone,
   to touch someone,
   to ask for something,
   to take something,
   to give something.

Whatever I make of this day,
whatever I become this day
I put into Your hands.

Anne Springsteen

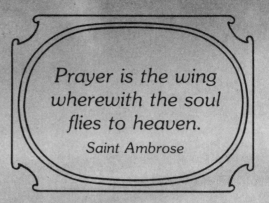

Prayer is the wing
wherewith the soul
flies to heaven.
Saint Ambrose

A Morning Prayer

The day returns
and brings us the petty round
of irritating concerns and duties.
Help us to play the man,
help us to perform them
with laughter and kind faces,
let cheerfulness abound with industry.
Give us to go blithely
on our business all this day,
bring us to our resting beds
weary and content and undishonored,
and grant us in the end
the gift of sleep.

Robert Louis Stevenson

Supplication

Give me a heart attuned to simple glories—
Leaf-dappled trails beneath my eager feet;

Bright little streams, bordered by slender willows;
The quiet hills, the meadows summer sweet.

Let me store deep in memory's chest the treasures
Of golden dawn and sunset, autumn trees;

    Lapis lazuli skies and silver moonlight.
    Perhaps sometime I may have need of these.

        And let me remember stars against that time
        That I may feel the need to touch a star

           And tulips for the day I may not go
           To find God in a spot where tulips are.

Lura Bailey Jones

Look to This Day!
—in hope

> Hope
> springs eternal
> in the human breast.
> *Alexander Pope*

Hope—of all ills that men endure,
the cheap and universal cure; the
captive's freedom and the sick
man's health, the lover's victory
and the beggar's wealth.

Crowley

Hope

Hope is a robin singing
On a rainy day;
He knows the sun will shine again
Though skies may now be gray.

Like the robin let us be,
Meet trouble with a smile;
And soon the sun will shine for us
In just a little while.

Beverly J. Anderson

Hope is a looking forward to
something with an earnest belief.
Often it means an expectancy of
light when one is still in darkness. I
like to think of it as the promise of
dawn to follow the night shadows.
Life takes new strength and meaning
where there is hope. Let us keep
this promise in our hearts.

Esther Baldwin York

9

The Unbroken String

Love and friendship, joy and sorrow,
these are the strings on which we play.
These are the notes that go to make
the varied music of the day.
With the passing of the years
the strings of life get frayed and thin—
and youth's high tones are touched
with sadness, like a muted violin.
But there is one undying thing,
one golden string that does not break:
the string of Hope.
We play upon it, and it never fails to wake
an echo in the weary spirit.
One sweet note fresh faith can bring.
For Hope is the music of the soul
played on the heart's unbroken string.

Patience Strong

Hope for Tomorrow

Hope thinks tomorrow
    will be brighter;
Faith knows,
And, knowing, is
    the surer of the two,
And makes it true.

But when the morrow
    lengthens into night
And shadows throng,
Hope, like another dawn,
    transfuses faith
And makes it strong.

Minnie Klemme

Look to This Day!
—in joy

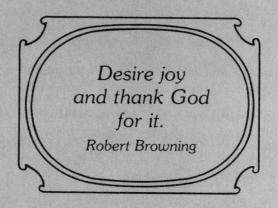

*Desire joy
and thank God
for it.*
Robert Browning

Oh, the wild joys of living!
    the leaping from rock up to rock,
The strong rending of boughs from the fir-tree,
    the cool silver shock
Of the plunge in a pool's living water,
    the hunt of the bear,
And the sultriness showing the lion
    is couched in his lair.

Robert Browning

The fruit of the spirit is . . . joy.

I have only the faintest hint as to what joy is.
I know we could not stand much of it at one time.
Perhaps, it is the few times in our life when
we know we are being
    who we should be
    when we should be
    where we should be.

"Joy." It is the most magical, haunting image I know.

Herbert B. Barks

13

The Waking

I strolled across
An open field;
The sun was out;
Heat was happy.

This way! This way!
The wren's throat shimmered,
Either to other,
The blossoms sang.

The stones sang,
The little ones did,
And flowers jumped
Like small goats.

A ragged fringe
Of daisies waved;
I wasn't alone
In a grove of apples.

Far in the wood
A nestling sighed;
The dew loosened
Its morning smells.

I came where the river
Ran over stones:
My ears knew
An early joy.

And all the waters
Of all the streams
Sang in my veins
That summer day.

Theodore Roethke

Afternoon
on a Hill

I will be the gladdest thing
  Under the sun!
I will touch a hundred flowers
And not pick one.

I will look at cliffs and clouds
  With quiet eyes,
Watch the wind bow down the grass,
  And the grass rise.

And when lights begin to show
  Up from the town,
I will mark which must be mine,
  And then start down.

Edna St. Vincent Millay

17

Look to This Day!
— in kindness

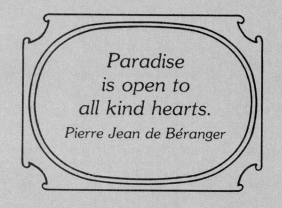

*Paradise
is open to
all kind hearts.*
Pierre Jean de Béranger

Oh, the comfort—the inexpressible comfort
    of feeling safe with a person,
Having neither to weigh thoughts,
Nor measure words — but pouring them
All right out — just as they are —
Chaff and grain together —
Certain that a faithful hand will
Take and sift them —
Keep what is worth keeping —
And with the breath of kindness
Blow the rest away.

           Dinah Maria Mulock Craik

Comfort

A Prayer

Grant us prudence in proportion to our power,
wisdom in proportion to our science, humaneness
in proportion to our wealth and might.

And bless our earnest will to help all races and
peoples to travel, in friendship with us,
Along the road to justice, liberty, and lasting
peace.

           Thomas Merton

Life's Ripples

A tiny pebble idly tossed
Into the placid stream,
With gentle splash it sinks from sight
And not again is seen.
But outward from that central spot
The circling ripples tend,
Who knows on what far distant shore
The spreading impulse ends?

And so it is with life itself;
A word we say—a deed we do
May take a moment of our time
And then be lost to view,
But ever onward it will go
And never lost shall be,
Until its widening mission done,
It joins infinity.

Edwin Roworth

Do all the good you can,
By all the means you can,
In all the ways you can,
In all the places you can,
At all the times you can,
To all the people you can,
As long as ever you can.

John Wesley

What do we live for, if it is not to make life less difficult to each other.

George Eliot

If you approach each new person you meet in a spirit of adventure, you will find yourself endlessly fascinated by the new channels of thought and experience and personality that you encounter.

Eleanor Roosevelt

A Mile with Me

O who will walk a mile with me
    Along life's merry way?
A comrade blithe and full of glee,
Who dares to laugh out loud and free,
And let his frolic fancy play,
Like a happy child, through the flowers gay
That fill the field and fringe the way
    Where he walks a mile with me.

And who will walk a mile with me
    Along life's weary way?
A friend whose heart has eyes to see
The stars shine out o'er the darkening lea,
And the quiet rest at the end o' the day,
A friend who knows, and dares to say,
The brave, sweet words that cheer the way
    Where he walks a mile with me.

With such a comrade, such a friend,
I fain would walk till journeys end,
Through summer sunshine, winter rain,
And then?—Farewell, we shall meet again!

Henry van Dyke

Look to This Day!
—in faith

High Adventure

As I have seen a child,
Round-eyed and innocent,
Leaving his treasured playthings piled
Where new adventure overtook,
Climb up a little staired ascent,
Holding in fear his parent's hand,
And, trepidant with fresh alarms
Yet gathering courage from each trustful look,
With utter confidence in a last command,
Fling himself laughing into his father's arms—

So I, another child,
Holding my Father's hand,
Now from my busy arts beguiled
By what He promises beyond,
Forgetting all that I have planned,
And pressing on with faith's sure sight
O'er rock and ridge, through mists and storms,
With confidence that swallows up despond,
From the last crag of life's most glorious height
Cast me exultant into my Father's arms.

A. W. Spalding

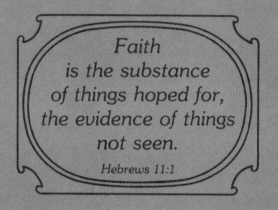

*Faith
is the substance
of things hoped for,
the evidence of things
not seen.*

Hebrews 11:1

The Voice of Faith

I have seen a curious child, who dwelt upon a tract
Of inland ground, applying to his ear
The convolutions of a smooth-lipped shell;
To which, in silence hushed, his very soul
Listened intensely; for from within were heard
Murmurings, whereby the monitor expressed
Mysterious union with its native sea.
Even such a shell the universe itself
Is to the ear of faith; and there are times,
I doubt not, when to you it doth impart
Authentic tidings of invisible things,
Of ebb and flow, and ever-enduring power,
And central peace, subsisting at the heart
Of endless agitation.

William Wordsworth

To Build Up Faith

God, please help me to build up my faith.

Let me understand that faith is not a blind acceptance, but a certain and reasonable knowledge.

Not a gift bestowed upon favored people, but a powerful conviction achieved through serious effort.

God, guide me to people who can encourage me in my faith. (Thank You for such people.)

Lead me to books that will enlighten and enhance my faith. (Thank You for such books.)

Show me works both human and divine that prove that You do exist and love us. Open my eyes to your many wonders.

Free my cluttered and limited mind from its confusions. Release it, refresh it, widen it so that into it may flow an appreciation of your vast, shining, limitless intelligence. (Thank You for that clearing and that comprehension now.)

Help me to practice my faith, for only through practice can it grow in me. Oh, God, remind me to reach you and understand you, and renew my faith through prayer.

Marjorie Holmes

How Manifold Are Thy Works

O Lord, how manifold are thy works!
In wisdom hast thou made them all;
the earth is full of thy creatures.

Thou hast made the moon to mark
the seasons;
the sun knows its time
for setting.
Thou makest darkness,
and it is night.

Yonder is the sea, great and wide,
which teems with things innumerable,
living things both small and great.

These all look to thee,
to give them their food in due season.

Bless the Lord, O my soul!
Praise the Lord!

Psalm 104:24-27, 35

Out in the Fields with God

The little cares that fretted me,
　I lost them yesterday
Among the fields above the sea,
　Among the winds that play,
Among the lowing of the herds,
　The rustling of the trees,
Among the singing of the birds,
　The humming of the bees.

The fears of what may come to pass,
　I cast them all away
Among the clover-scented grass,
　Among the new-mown hay,
Among the rustling of the corn,
　Where drowsy poppies nod,
Where ill thoughts die and good are born,
　Out in the fields with God.

Author Unknown

Evensong

The embers of the day are red
Beyond the murky hill.
The kitchen smokes;
The bed in the darkling
House is spread:
The great sky darkens overhead,
And the great woods are shrill.
So far have I been led,
Lord, by Thy will:
So far have I followed,
Lord, and wondered still.
The breeze from the
Embalmed land
Blows sudden towards the shore,
And claps my cottage door.
I hear the signal, Lord—
I understand.
The night at Thy command
Comes.
I will eat and sleep and
Will not question more.

Robert Louis Stevenson

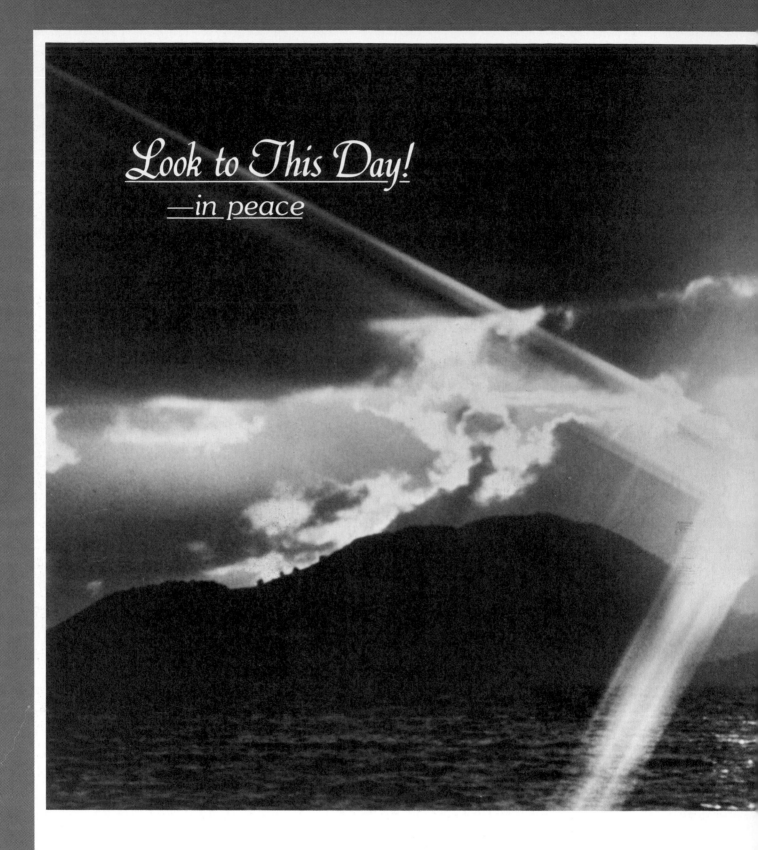

Look to This Day!
—in peace

One Day at a Time

Ralph Waldo Emerson

Finish every day and be done with it.
You have done what you could.
Some blunders and absurdities no doubt crept in;
forget them as soon as you can.

Tomorrow is a new day;
begin it well and serenely
and with too high a spirit to be cumbered
with your old nonsense.

This day is all that is good and fair.
It is too dear,
with its hopes and invitations,
to waste a moment on the yesterdays.

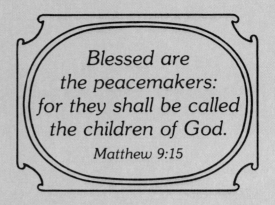

*Blessed are
the peacemakers:
for they shall be called
the children of God.*

Matthew 9:15

A Morning Wish

The sun is just rising on the morning of another
day. What can I wish that this day may bring me?
Nothing that shall make the world or others
poorer, nothing at the expense of other men, but
just those few things which in their coming do
not stop with me but touch me, rather, as they
pass and gather strength.

A few friends who understand me, and yet
remain my friends . . .

A mind unafraid to travel, even though the trail
be not blazed.

A sight of the eternal hills and the unresting sea
and of something beautiful which the hand of
man has made.

A sense of humor and the power to laugh. A little
leisure with nothing to do.

A few moments of quiet, silent meditation. The
sense of the presence of God.

And the patience to wait for the coming of these
things, with the wisdom to know them when they
come, and the wit not to change this morning
wish of mine.

Walter Reid Hunt

Peace

Peace is looking at a child
    With eyelids closed in sleep
And knowing that the love of God
    Is constant, true and deep.

Peace is gazing into depths
    Of water, cool and clear,
And knowing fast within your heart
    That God is ever near.

Peace is hearing birds that sing
    In harmony of voice,
And knowing that you, too, can live
    With God's own way your choice.

Peace is living day by day
    With His own company,
So you will have within your soul
    Divine tranquility.

Mildred Spires Jacobs

Purpose

Dear Lord, may others find in me
A pool of cool tranquility;
A quiet resting place to find
New strength of heart and peace of mind.

May all who stop within my gate
Find solace here; exchange the hate
For love that ever-widening dwells
Outside the circle of themselves.

And may I have the listening ear
That helps dispel all doubt and fear.
In days of dark uncertainty,
Lord, place an inner light in me.

Lord, should my inner light be low,
Help Thy unfailing grace to grow,
That all who come to me with care
May see Thy love reflected there.

Margaret Freer

I Will Not Hurry

I will not hurry through this day!
Lord, I will listen by the way,
To humming bees and singing birds,
To speaking trees and friendly words;
And, for the moments in between
Seek glimpses of Thy great Unseen.

I will not hurry through this day;
I will take time to think and pray;
I will look up into the sky,
Where fleecy clouds and swallows fly;
And, somewhere in the day, maybe
I will catch whispers, Lord, from Thee!

Ralph Spaulding Cushman

Possession

I always owned the sky; the sky was mine
From the moment I first looked up at it, and felt
All the enormous tender brilliance shine
Into my wondering heart, where it has dwelt
Unceasingly. I own uncounted millions
Of stars, though using only two or three,
And as for clouds, of course, I've many trillions,
And the sun is my peculiar property.
My ownership of sky does not preclude
Others enjoying it; I'm glad to share
My glad possession of infinitude,
But any who come between us must beware,
Since, whether lightning-lashed or rainbow-lit,
The sky belongs to me, and I to it.

Jane Merchant

Look to This Day!
—in beauty

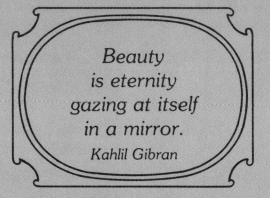

*Beauty
is eternity
gazing at itself
in a mirror.*
Kahlil Gibran

God's World

O world, I cannot hold thee close enough!
　　Thy winds, thy wide grey skies!
　　Thy mists, that roll and rise!
Thy woods, this autumn day, that ache and sag
And all but cry with colour! That gaunt crag
To crush! To lift the lean of that black bluff!
World, World, I cannot get thee close enough!

Long have I known a glory in it all,
　　But never knew I this;
　　Here such a passion is
As stretcheth me apart —Lord, I do fear
Thou'st made the world too beautiful this year;
My soul is all but out of me —let fall
No burning leaf; prithee, let no bird call.

Edna St. Vincent Millay

Pied Beauty

Glory be to God for dappled things—
For skies of couple-colour as a brinded cow;
For rose-moles all in stipple upon trout that swim;
Fresh-firecoal chestnut-falls; finches' wings;
Landscape plotted and pieced—fold, fallow, and plough;
And all trades, their gear and tackle and trim.

All things counter, original, spare, strange;
Whatever is fickle, freckled (who knows how?)
With swift, slow; sweet, sour; adazzle, dim;
He fathers-forth whose beauty is past change:
Praise him.

Gerard Manley Hopkins

Natural Beauty

The most natural beauty in the world
is honesty and moral truth;
for all beauty is truth.
True features make the beauty of a face;
and true proportions the beauty of architecture;
as true measures that of harmony and music.
In poetry, which is all fable,
truth still is the perfection.

Anthony A. Cooper

Barter

Life has loveliness to sell,
    All beautiful and splendid things,
Blue waves whitened on a cliff,
    Soaring fire that sways and sings,
And children's faces looking up
Holding wonder like a cup.

Life has loveliness to sell,
    Music like a curve of gold,
Scent of pine trees in the rain,
    Eyes that love you, arms that hold,
And for your spirit's still delight,
Holy thoughts that star the night.

Spend all you have for loveliness,
    Buy it and never count the cost;
For one white singing hour of peace
    Count many a year of strife well lost,
And for a breath of ecstasy
Give all you have been, or could be.

Sara Teasdale

Beauty Is Abroad

Beauty is abroad in the land today,
In the wild flowers blooming along the way,
In the changing green in the light on the trees.
Its voice is heard in the whispering breeze,
In the rippling stream as it glides along,
In the happy notes of the bluebird's song.
It climbs a hill, glides over the ridge
And spans a stream at a rustic bridge.
Oh, beauty is abroad in the land today
In many guises along the way.

Beauty is abroad in the land today . . .
It smiles and beckons along the way.
It dances gaily in a field of flowers
And plays hide-and-seek in leafy bowers.
It's flung like a robe over pastures green,
It rides on a cloud or a pale moonbeam.
It's hiding deep in the heart of a rose,
It lurks in the field where the violet grows.
Oh, beauty is abroad in the land today . . .
And it's forever there beside the way.

Anna Vallance

The Rhodora

In May, when sea-winds pierced our solitudes,
I found the fresh Rhodora in the woods,
Spreading its leafless blooms in a damp nook,
To please the desert and the sluggish brook.

The purple petals, fallen in the pool,
Made the black water with their beauty gay;
Here might the redbird come his plumes to cool,
And court the flower that cheapens his array.

Rhodora! if the sages ask thee why
This charm is wasted on the earth and sky,
Tell them, dear, that if eyes were made for seeing,
Then Beauty is its own excuse for being:

Why thou wert there, O rival of the rose!
I never thought to ask, I never knew:
But, in my simple ignorance, suppose
The self-same Power that brought me there brought you.

Ralph Waldo Emerson

Look to This Day!

—in love

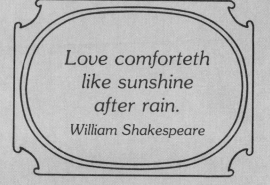

Love comforteth
like sunshine
after rain.
William Shakespeare

Answer to a Child's Question

Do you ask what the birds say?
  The sparrow, the dove,
The linnet and thrush say,
  "I love and I love!"
In the winter they're silent—
  the wind is so strong;
What it says, I don't know,
  but it sings a loud song.
But green leaves, and blossoms,
  and sunny warm weather,
And singing, and loving—
  all come back together.
But the lark is so brimful
  of gladness and love,
The green fields below him,
  the blue sky above,
That he sings, and he sings;
  and for ever sings he—
"I love my Love,
  and my Love loves me!"

Samuel Taylor Coleridge

49

Perfect Love

Perfect love has this advantage in it,
that it leaves the possessor of it
nothing farther to desire.
There is one object (at least)
in which the soul finds absolute content,
for which it seeks to live,
or dares to die.
The heart has, as it were,
filled up the moulds of the imagination.
The truth of passion keeps pace with
and outvies the extravagance of mere language.
There are no words so fine,
no flattery so soft,
that there is not a sentiment beyond them,
that it is impossible to express,
at the bottom of the heart where true love is.
What idle sounds the common phrases,
adorable creature, angel, divinity, are!
What a proud reflection it is to have
a feeling answering to all these,
rooted in the breast, unalterable, unutterable,
to which all other feelings are light and vain!
Perfect love reposes on the object of its choice,
like the halcyon on the wave;
and the air of heaven is around it.

William Hazlitt

Miracle of Love

This is the miracle that happens
every time to those who really love:
the more they give, the more they possess
of that precious nourishing love
from which flowers and children
have their strength
and which could help all human beings
if they would take it
without doubting.

Rainer Maria Rilke

A Day

What does it take to make a day?
A lot of love along the way:
It takes a morning and a noon,
A father's voice, a mother's croon;
It takes some task to challenge all
The powers that a man may call
His own: the powers of mind and limb;
A whispered word of love; a hymn
Of hope—a comrade's cheer—
A baby's laughter and a tear;
It takes a dream, a hope, a cry
Of need from some soul passing by;
A sense of brotherhood and love;
A purpose sent from God above;
It takes a sunset in the sky,
The stars of night, the winds that sigh;
It takes a breath of scented air,
A mother's kiss, a baby's prayer.
That is what it takes to make a day;
A lot of love along the way.

William L. Stidger

53

Moon
Compasses

I stole forth dimly in the dripping pause
Between two downpours to see what there was.
And a masked moon had spread down compass rays
To a cone mountain in the midnight haze,
As if the final estimate were hers;
And as it measured in her calipers,
The mountain stood exalted in its place.
So love will take between the hands a face . . .

Robert Frost

Love

Love is the only bow on life's dark cloud.
It is the Morning and the Evening Star.
It shines upon the cradle of the babe,
and sheds its radiance upon the quiet tomb.
It is the mother of Art,
inspirer of poet, patriot and philosopher.
It is the air and light of every heart,
builder of every home,
kindler of every fire on every hearth.
It was the first to dream of immortality.
It fills the world with melody,
for Music is the voice of Love.
Love is the magician, the enchanter,
that changes worthless things to joy,
and makes right royal kings and queens of common clay.
It is the perfume of the wondrous flower—the heart—
and without that sacred passion, that divine swoon,
we are less than beasts;
but with it, earth is heaven
and we are gods.

Robert G. Ingersoll

Look to This Day!
—in imagination

They can
because they think
they can.
Virgil

Dream-Pedlary

If there were dreams to sell,
  What would you buy?
Some cost a passing bell;
  Some a light sigh,
That shakes from Life's fresh crown
Only a rose-leaf down.
If there were dreams to sell,
Merry and sad to tell,
And the crier rang the bell,
  What would you buy?

A cottage lone and still,
  With bowers nigh,
Shadowy, my woes to still,
  Until I die.
Such pearl from Life's fresh crown
Fain would I shake me down.
Were dreams to have at will,
This would best heal my ill,
  This would I buy.

Thomas L. Beddoes

My Heart's
in the Highlands

My heart's in the Highlands, my heart is not here;
My heart's in the Highlands a-chasing the deer;
A-chasing the wild deer, and following the roe,
My heart's in the Highlands, wherever I go.
Farewell to the Highlands, farewell to the North,
The birth place of Valour, the country of Worth,
Wherever I wander, wherever I rove,
The hills of the Highlands for ever I love.

Farewell to the mountains high cover'd with snow;
Farewell to the straths and green vallies below;
Farewell to the forests and wild hanging woods;
Farewell to the torrents and loud pouring floods.
My heart's in the Highlands, my heart is not here,
My heart's in the Highlands a-chasing the deer;
Chasing the wild deer, and following the roe;
My heart's in the Highlands, wherever I go.

Robert Burns

Hold Fast Your Dreams

Louise Driscoll

Hold fast your dreams!
Within your heart
Keep one still, secret spot
Where dreams may go,
And, sheltered so,
May thrive and grow
Where doubt and fear are not.

O keep a place apart,
Within your heart,
For little dreams to go!

Think still of lovely things that are not true.
Let wish and magic work at will in you.
Be sometimes blind to sorrow. Make believe!
Forget the calm that lies
In disillusioned eyes.
Though we all know that we must die,
Yet you and I
May walk like gods and be
Even now at home in immortality.
We see so many ugly things—
Deceits and wrongs and quarrelings;

We know, alas! we know
How quickly fade
The color in the west,
The bloom upon the flower,
The bloom upon the breast
And youth's blind hour.
Yet keep within your heart
A place apart
Where little dreams may go,
May thrive and grow.
Hold fast—hold fast your dreams!

I wandered lonely as a cloud
   That floats on high o'er vales and hills,
When all at once I saw a crowd,
   A host of golden daffodils
Beside the lake, beneath the trees,
Fluttering and dancing in the breeze.

Continuous as the stars that shine
   And twinkle on the Milky Way,
They stretched in never-ending line
   Along the margin of a bay:
Ten thousand saw I, at a glance,
Tossing their heads in sprightly dance.

I Wandered
Lonely
As a Cloud

The waves beside them danced, but they
   Outdid the sparkling waves in glee;
A poet could not but be gay
   In such a jocund company;
I gazed—and gazed—but little thought
What wealth the show to me had brought.

For oft, when on my couch I lie,
   In vacant or in pensive mood,
They flash upon that inward eye
   Which is the bliss of solitude;
And then my heart with pleasure fills,
And dances with the daffodils.

William Wordsworth

Look to This Day!
—in wisdom

> *Wisdom*
> *is oft'times nearer*
> *when we stoop*
> *than when we soar.*
> William Wordsworth

O World

O world, thou choosest not the better part!
It is not wisdom to be only wise,
And on the inward vision close the eyes,
But it is wisdom to believe the heart.
Columbus found a world, and had no chart,
Save one that faith deciphered in the skies;
To trust the soul's invincible surmise
Was all his science and his only art.
Our knowledge is a torch of smoky pine
That lights the pathway but one step ahead
Across a void of mystery and dread.
Bid, then, the tender light of faith to shine
By which alone the mortal heart is led
Unto the thinking of the thought divine.

George Santayana

But the wisdom from above is first
pure, then peaceable, gentle, open
to reason, full of mercy and good fruits,
without uncertainty or insincerity.

James 3:17

For This Is Wisdom

For this is wisdom; to love, to live,
To take what fate, or the gods, may give,
To ask no question, to make no prayer,
To kiss the lips and caress the hair,
Speed passion's ebb as you greet its flow,
To have —to hold —and —in time —let go!

Laurence Hope

Flower in the Crannied Wall

Flower in the crannied wall,
I pluck you out of the crannies,
I hold you here, root and all, in my hand,
Little flower—but *if* I could understand
What you are, root and all, and all in all,
I should know what God and man is.

Alfred, Lord Tennyson

For Wisdom

Endow me with a thirst for truth,
Deny me self-content,
And make me useful in this world
Until my life is spent.

Give me a faith that's strong and sure,
Above all temporal things.
Give me a sense of humor to
Offset life's tiresome stings.

Give me a humble spirit, Lord,
Where wisdom will take root,
And help me then to cultivate
Each tender, budding shoot.

And finally, Lord, make me sincere
In all I do and say,
That I may build an inner fort
Which nothing can dismay.

Viney Wilder

As for man, his days are like grass;
he flourishes like a flower of the field;
for the wind passes over it, and it is gone,
and its place knows it no more.
But the steadfast love of the Lord
is from everlasting to everlasting.

Psalm 103:15-17

What Is the Grass?

A child said What is the grass?
Fetching it to me with full hands,
How could I answer the child?
I do not know what it is any more than he.

I guess it must be the flag of my disposition,
Out of hopeful green stuff woven.

Or I guess it is the handkerchief of the Lord,
A scented gift and remembrancer designedly dropt,
Bearing the owner's name someway in the corners,
That we may see and remark, and say Whose?

Walt Whitman

Look to This Day!
—for life

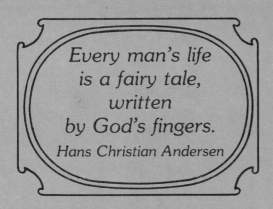

Every man's life
is a fairy tale,
written
by God's fingers.
Hans Christian Andersen

The Road Not Taken

Two roads diverged in a yellow wood,
And sorry I could not travel both
And be one traveler, long I stood
And looked down one as far as I could
To where it bent in the undergrowth;

Then took the other, as just as fair,
And having perhaps the better claim,
Because it was grassy and wanted wear;
Though as for that, the passing there
Had worn them really about the same,

And both that morning equally lay
In leaves no step had trodden black.
Oh, I kept the first for another day!
Yet knowing how way leads on to way,
I doubted if I should ever come back.

I shall be telling this with a sigh
Somewhere ages and ages hence:
Two roads diverged in a wood, and I—
I took the one less traveled by,
And that has made all the difference.

Robert Frost

Two Carefree Days

There are two days in the week about
which and upon which I never worry.
Two carefree days, kept sacredly free
from fear and apprehension.
One of these days is
    Yesterday.

Yesterday with all its cares and frets,
with all its pains and aches,
all its faults,
and its mistakes and blunders,
has passed forever beyond the reach
of my recall.
I cannot undo an act that I wrought.
I cannot unsay a word that I said
on Yesterday.
All that it holds of my life,
of wrong, regret and sorrow
is in the hands
of the Mighty Love
that can bring honey out of the rock
and sweet waters out of the bitterest desert.

And the other day I do not worry about is
    Tomorrow.
Tomorrow with all its possible adversities,
its burdens, its perils,
its large promise
and poor performance,
its failures and mistakes,
is as far beyond the reach
of my mastery
as its dead sister,
    Yesterday.

Robert J. Burdette

For Great Moments

We give thee thanks, O God,

For great moments of joy and strength that come to us when by a strong and special movement of grace we are able to perform some act of pure and disinterested love.

For the clean fire of that love which floods the soul and cleanses the whole man and leaves us filled with an unexpected lightness and freedom for action.

For the moment of pure prayer which not only establishes order in the soul, but even fortifies us against physical weariness and brings us a new lease on life itself.

Glory be to Thee for thy precious gift!

Thomas Merton

It is a great deal better to live a holy life than to talk about it. Lighthouses do not ring bells and fire cannons to call attention to their shining. They just shine!

Dwight L. Moody

All Times Are His Seasons

We ask our daily bread, and God never says, You should have come yesterday. He never says, You must come again tomorrow. But "today if you will hear His voice," today He will hear you. If some king of the earth have so large an extent of dominion in north and south as that he hath winter and summer together in his dominions, so large an extent of east and west as that he hath day and night together in his dominions, much more hath God mercy and judgment together. He brought light out of darkness, not out of a lesser light. He can bring thy summer out of winter though thou have no spring.

Though in the ways of fortune, or misunderstanding, or conscience, thou have been benighted till now, wintered and frozen, clouded and eclipsed, damp and benumbed, smothered and stupefied till now, now God comes to thee, not as in dawning of the day, not as in the bud of the spring, but as the sun at noon, to banish all shadows; as the sheaves in harvest, to fill all penuries. All occasions invite His mercies, and all times are His season.

God made sun and moon to distinguish seasons, and day and night; and we cannot have the fruits of the earth but in their seasons. But God hath made no decrees to distinguish the seasons of His mercies. In Paradise the fruits were ripe the first minute, and in Heaven it is always autumn, His mercies are ever in their maturity.

John Donne

There Was a Child
Went Forth

There was a child went forth every day;
And the first object he looked upon, the object he became;
And that object became part of him for the day, or a certain
    part of the day, or for many years, or stretching cycles
    of years:
The early lilacs became part of this child;

And the apple-trees covered with blossoms, and the fruit
    afterward, and wood-berries, and the commonest weeds
    by the road;

The blow, the quick loud word, the tight bargain, the crafty
    lure,
The family usages, the language, the company, the furniture
    —the yearning and swelling heart;

The doubts of day-time and the doubts of night-time—the
    curious whether and how,
Whether that which appears so is so, or is it all flashes and
    specks?
Men and women crowding fast in the streets—if they are
    not flashes and specks, what are they?

These became part of that child who went forth every day,
    and who now goes, and will always go forth every day.

Walt Whitman

Day!

Faster and more fast,
O'er night's brim, day boils at last;
Boils, pure gold, o'er the cloud-cap's brim
Where spurting and suppressed it lay,
For not a froth-flake touched the rim
Of yonder gap in the solid gray
Of the eastern cloud, an hour away;
But forth one wavelet, then another, curled,
Till the whole sunrise, not to be suppressed,
Rose, reddened, and its seething breast
Flickered in bounds, grew gold,
Then overflowed the world.

Robert Browning

Look to This Day!

in prayer, hope, joy,
kindness, faith, peace
beauty, love, imagination
and in wisdom.

Look to This Day for Life!